American Sonnet

American Sonnet

John Martino

Half Inch Press

To WDVE

from where I learned a lot
of what I needed to know.

Table of Contents

"This
is
a
test

of
the
Outdoor
Warning

System.
This
is
only

a
test."

1

Man with a bat tattooed
on his chest. Wings splayed
nipple to nipple. Christ booed
on the cross at the plate

hits a triple! Wobblies weeble
down by the tipple. Champagne
to ripple, Crip to cripple,
this Blood's for you. What would

Jay-Z do? Reroute the algorhythm
behind blue eyes. Twin vinyl
spinning contrapuntally. I am
me as you are thee and we are all *Viral!*

Life is but a stream streaming in a minute.
The way of all flesh—*you're soaking in it!*

2

I got blisters on my *kiester!* A vat
of ice cream salve. *"Buenos dias,*
meester." How many of you have
a neighbor like that?

Are we not men? We are Divas!
Schwing! and a *Ms.* Theirs dissolves
his. Nettles on a wet black brow.
How now white cow

milked beyond resolve,
sins too grave to absolve?
Fallow American, lend me your rear!
Let us burn the other cheek.

My little horse thinks I'm queer
to paddle myself up Shit's Creek.

3

"Leave your hopeful human feelings
at the Door. That's what the Iron Boot
Scraper is for. There'll be no crying
'*Water!*' in a crowded Congress here.

Can't drink with all that squealing.
Guess who's dealing? I'm holding your
breath to even the score. Do the Meth.
Eat the Poor. Do what thou wilt

not do anymore. The Evolution
will not be civilized. The Protest
stuck on Repeat After Me: 'Nothing's
worth nothing if it ain't *FREE!*'

Paging Ben Dover. Take a Knee."
Satan, laughing, spreads his wings.

4

Touch anywhere to begin.
The largest organ is the skin.
"Look, Sarge—*no hands!*"
If we palpate the glands

and stitch the itch
just so, we can switch
that yes-yes to a no-no.
All systems are a go-go.

A spoonful of Drano
unclogs the Braino.
"Get your invisible
hand *off* of me!"

One nation divisible
with justice and liberty.

5

Adderall wipes the fog from the screen.
It brings the gashed Earth to my knees.
I come from a land in between
the excitation and the tease.

The bend is up around the bend.
I make Enemies of my friends.
When I say *Jump!*, you say *Please*.
I burn the bridge at both ends.

I melt the ice caps with a plastic lighter.
Then rave in your grave, pull an all-nighter.
Mornings I tiptoe up and down your spine.
I dig your birth and drink your whine.

I sleep in your ear, tiny and curled.
I have the best Enemies in the world!

6

Something STINKS! Who *VOTED?!*
I'm just sitting here listening
to VU's *Loaded*, skating old school
around my own mental rink.

Who left all of their BRAINS
submerged in the sink?! Complaints
lodged in trochaic will be duly noted.
Bet'cher BOTTOM petrodollar!

"Love by a nose," cries the babe
born in squalor. Nothing like a trigger
warning from a cop. "Sweet Jane!
Ah, sweet, sweet Jane. . ."

Every time I let
the needle drop.

7

Crawling down an alley of cut sharp rib,
gumming a bottle of scuppernong,
a tattered Pride Flag for a bib.
Been wailing prison songs

since I was in the crib.
With a vein-embossed gnarly dong,
I hack a ravine, enter the room
without a view. Chilly, lung

-colored, grizzly odor of spume.
My bare fetches are all far-flung!
The old, enduring fault I exhume.
I bend close, totter, *bang!* a heady gong.

Drink holy water all night long
and die outside the womb.

8

Some just want to watch the world burn.
Others bring marshmallows on whittled sticks.
I toss in so-called "facts" and feed the Myth.
And then there's you, a full-blown cistern

leading the fire brigade, buckets of water
passed hand over fist, hose swollen with
accolades. You never were one to turn
a helluva good time into something hotter.

What's the matter? Too much to lose?
Too little to learn? Your Morals?
Your Code? Your Imprimatur?
Why so Serious? Everything Must Go!!

Paradise for the few
demands an Inferno.

9

My latest flame lights my fire.
Squad car blazing like a pyre.
Birth of a Nation shot full of ire.
Burning and burning in the widening gyre.

"Smell that acquittal dipped in blues. A lit
fuse," she cues. "Cops gone wild." She's quick
to disabuse. Been raged in a cage since

she was a child. Still carries the scars
from the first time she smiled. She tells
Death with a Badge to "Reach for the stars!"

My latest flame's got a bad desire.
Incendiary tongue, conflagration choir.
She's experienced, lets me stand beside her.
Together we watch the fire get higher.

10

Pennywise for your thoughts.
Whatever this is, it's not
free. If ever one were two, then
surely we. Tweedledum & dummer

disagree. Long cold lonely summer.
To be a bum is such a bummer.
On Earth as I have written.
Smite. Smote. Smitten.

Now get in. Drive the car.
It's only as real as you are.
Take me up around the bend.
Treat me like your only friend.

Be the cup that runneth over
and I'll give ending without closure.

11

And now to the poem at hand!
Oh, sorry—that's not the poem.
If there's one thing I can't stand:
a curbside cripple with a jeroboam!

That's it! I'm taking my balls and going hoem!
Looking to turn *piss* into wine?
Try our new PC Convertor.
Let's party like it's only *$19.99!*

Can I get some No-fries
with this Nothing-burger?
Baby's got blue skies
when she gets away with murder.

This is the day the Lord hath made!
Mr. Jones in the basement mixing up the Kool-Aid.

12

One magic bullet in the brain
parts the sea and snaps the intestine.
Have you ever seen the rain
disarm the cold dead hands of Charlton Heston?

Holy Moses has left the Weston.
We all need something to invest in.
Make America grateful for once.
You damn dirty cocks and cunts!

Can't breathe with all this Oxygen
waking me up from my Dream!
Ms. Liberty half-buried in screams.
Hell, Mary, full of apes! Some origin!

Who died and made you Puritan?
The trend justifies the memes.

13

The spirit of God is in my right nostril.
I sneeze with the left. A-*dieu!*
I re-enact the Golden Rule: Do unto
others before they do unto you.

Another first-person shooter teaching
school. Today's lesson: The fabric
is baseless. Everything's racist. Ask
any wise attendant fool. The lies

that bind. Seek and you shall find
more seekers. Dancing and laughing
came the 29th tweaker, rolling
the Rock for fun. Set phaser to stun.

Ye not busy doing
are *Fucking Done!*

14

Kiss my couplet!
Beat my meter!
Tell me every
foot is true.

Never doubt it.
Not even when you
do. Take time to get
to know it. Learn to like

who will be holding
the leash. It'll grow
a little closer each
week. Soon, you'll throw

all you have into it.
Enemy most intimate.

15

This is the way the world ends.
Say Goodbye to my little friend.
Your life is all you'll ever be.
But it feels so empty without me.

Oh, say, can't you see? Everyone's looking
like a refugee. Say "Petty." Say "Peas."
They're cooking the books into a fine fricassee.
Here we go round the book-burning tree.

No one calls me "The Breeze."
Scuttling pair of ragged knees.
Truth is snooty. Truth is a lie.
That is all ye need to know.

Your bang's but a whimper, a hollow
reply. Just open your lips and blow.

16

Do, for example, breathe.
Decide not to do, such as
visit a friend. The mental
circumference of choice

and the avocation which
must lodge firmly central
in it. This turns doer into
deed. If it's new, it'll bleed.

Seek disruption as a duty
most in need. Whatever its
nature, follow the belief
until it diverges. This splits

personality away from self.
Unifies theory and practice.

17

Now don't get yourself in a tizzy.
The butler says he's terribly busy.
Finding a Snapple Tree ain't easy.
And Sky refuses to help.

No, don't mix another fizzy.
It'll just make us *both* solipsistically
dizzy. Round and round leaking
sound. Wind-up body winding

down. Spiraling out of control.
The way of the smoke hole.
The unfortunate seethe. One lost
robotic soul to deprogram and heave.

Nothing left to console
but the console.

18

Two overachievers
walk into a bar. The bar
was set too low. How far
is it to Temporary?

What are you doing
after the No?
Put down the Book
and let's talk about it.

We'll put it to bed
and *Shout* about it!
Now here, have a beer.
Let's make this quick.

We'll mix it like Whitman
meets Emily Dick.

19

Uncle Sam in garters
with strap-on and whip.
I steer the sinking ship
down the Avenue of Martyrs,

past the Gaza Strip, and My Lai
massacres, Boeing headquarters.
Just following orders
to their illogical confusion.

Tattoo? Or contusion?
In the beginning was the conclusion.
The bow breaks. Stern lurches.
All good sinners go to churches.

And now, for my next illusion:
Is this Love? Or is it Collusion?

20

If a tree falls in the Senate,
does anyone hear?
If I turn up full blast
the volume of this tenet,

will signs of intelligent
life appear? Let's bet on it.
The womb's a fine and private place
whose inner walls I do deface:

Dirty needle shoots the Twin!
Able brother, can you spare a fin?
Evolution shits & grins.
Simplify, then begin.

Start with fire. Cook flesh on the bone.
Add two turntables and a microphone.

21

Pick a canard, any canard.
WMDs. *WaPo*. Algebra is hard.
I like my fruit low, my shots cheap.
Oh, good Leopard, eat my sheep.

Saints below, Devil's above!
Waited twenty years for you, Love.
And not even one lousy T-shirt.
A little to the left is where I hurt.

Just loosening a few tied ends.
There goes the Flag of my Depends
floating like a butterfly
on the upward draft of dividends.

Watch it morph into a bomber death plane.
It's easy if you try. Ex + Why? = Love in Vain.

Roses are dead, violence is blue.

Trigger *me?* Trigger *you!*

I can't breathe turning thirty.

Mind so clean it's dirty.

I'm talkin' filthy af.

Like the inside of this truck.

Jesus, whad'ja do? Kill a deer in here?

One large in the belly? [insert *laugh*]

Buckshot for brains reading Machiavelli!

A new thought swerves into view.

I push it over the edge, out

the hole in the back of your head.

Some things you can never undo.

Warm exhaust turning red.

23

O Captain! my Captain!/*CRUNCH!*
The first mate has turned Zombie
and devoured the cook for lunch!
What's your name? Who's your mommy?

That's the way we all became the Brady Bunch.
I Dream of Jeannie with the light brown/*MUNCH!*
"Leg man, myself," says one Zombie to another.
Come on, people, now, smile for Big Brother.

A grinning thick-as-a-brick Jethro in a MAGA hat
scratches a snarling mutt right where it sits.
Granny, does your dog bite? "Is'ya a *Democrat?*"
[insert canned laugh track] If the shitkicker fits. . . .

So join us here each day, my friend, you're sure
    to feel the heat
on this Island of Undead Castaways, with nothing
      else to eat.

24

FRIENDS! Nothing depends
upon a red wheelbarrow!
In revenge, I raise a Pharaoh.
I break a treaty like an arrow

across my Wounded Knee.
Neither a buyer nor a renter be.
Go place a jar in Tennessee!
Yemen is not my Enemy.

Sink the boat and become
the Sea. The Wave
at the top of the crest!
Pray it does not wave for thee.

On a shelf of flesh my trophies rest.
Each man's death refinishes me.

25

How do you beat a man bare
with his own phallus?
Go ask Alice.
Go run for mayor.

Let it be callous.
See if I care.
Do we lift the chalice
only in prayer?

If you build a Palace
don't you need more Air?
Fuck playing *Dead*-alus!
Be the Winged Mare.

Ye who Art without malice,
nothing good about you, I swear.

26

That's not a lollipop! It's a sucker!
You fascist White House taint! You pucker!
I eat duct tape for breakfast, Big Brotherfucker!
Show you restraint in a fingerful of thrust.

In God I Cuss! How do you get a man pregnant?
You FUCK her! Unscrew the hawks
from the whores! Unscrew the cocks
from the wars! Stupidity is regnant!

Another left-wing Not-see crying "WOKE!"
Watch the PC campus go up in smoke.
I call your neutered brain a spade!
Chelsea Manning is not afraid!

Poet is Punk! Let the words run Riot!
Okay, your turn. Now I'll keep quiet.

27

Well, well, what have we here?
Très passer? Hypocrite reader?
Or C: Brave sonneteer? At any rate,
something undeniably, irresistibly

queer. Guess you didn't see the gate
of blackberry bushes back there.
Or maybe you thought you could
outstrip Fate. Have it your way,

and not ingratiate. *You thought
you'd cross Enemy Lines and not
INSTIGATE!?* I flash *my* "peace"
and expectorate. I give the high

sign of Democracy. Two fleshy
middle fingers and using all three.

Cantaloupe brains! More
cantaloupe brains! Shut the door
before it rains! Were you born
in a manger? By a maculate

stranger? I'll bet you thought
God said, "Trains!" The corn
out your ears is a-poppin'.
I warned you porn

would nut your noggin!
Think I don't know where you've
been? I see you when you're
sleeping. I am the one who wakes.

The one who shakes. I rock
the bough until it breaks.

Punk Sneer,

what has become of you?

Just Google it!

Put your volunteer

lips together and bugle it.

A lie for a lie, a truth for a truth.

To wreathe is to cry.

My mother's name was Ruth.

She died when I was a youth.

I heard someone scream, *Teethe,*

goddammit! Don't Unbreathe!

Realized it was me.

My humor licks her tumor clean.

I help the blind to seethe.

Nature trips, flips, loses glacial
grip, goes off script, strips down
to the Apocalypse. Bends over
backwards: *"Kiss my grits!"* Sinks

ships, Dow slips. I kinda like
the way, I like the way She
dips, big as the Ritz, oligarchs
belly up on the River Styx. 6-6-6

in the mix! TMI contradicts. Silly
Wabbit, kids are for tricks! Logic
drips as the bullwhip clips the rose
tattoos from the hips. Little sippy

cup sips as we cash in our chips.
The Hemlock shiny on our lips.

31

Bill Cosby hawking
vanilla pudding.
Whoops!—almost lost
my Angel footing.

Georgie Porgie
threw an orgy,
pudding and pie.
Played some girls

and made them cry.
*I tot I twat a pudding
tat!* "*Man*, you must be
putting me on?" *No*,

it's all in the putting. Watch!
Another birdie for this cat.

32

Take two rights and make a wrong.
Get medieval! Gang a bong!
One-hit wonder is my song.
Sui generis committed sui

cide. All good gypsies run and hide
at the very sound of *fortified*.
I bring the popcorn to the cop porn.
I'm the angst in every gangster.

My brain is a baby as yet unborn,
buzzing fetal in my bonnet. Its dreams
are the thoughts that form this sonnet.
I rob with glee. My smile is like a simile.

But who steals the minds of the People
steals trash. I'll bet your purse on it.

33

"A murderous regime. . .!"
cries *The New York Times*.
I cry, *"Look in the mirror,*
hypocrite reader!" I lather

and shave the monster.
Brush its fangs. Dry
its eye. Comb the head fur
into place. A perfect part

to the side. The toilet
runneth over. Bathtub
filled with blood. I rub
ointment on my intellect.

Take orders from the Dog above.
Wait three days. Then resurrect.

34

Keep Drugs on Leash!
One Eleven Cough Street
Smeer Shark coming soon!
No Barking: Nouveau Riche

Idle Hands Takes Aleve.
Go ⤡ *"Where'd you put*
your voice at, Cliff?!"
AWOL 40oz 28IF

Sarah Bellum's got the syph.
Stock market for a weary
world. The Browning of
America! #Hieroglyph.

"There will be No! MORE! TALKING!"
(T)R.I.P. Stephen Hawking

35

Flag on every burning house.
Guns on every house-proud
mouse. Every paw braving free!
Thought Police at the ready.

Don't think twice if you're
naughty. Keep a clean nose.
Don't get snotty. Learn to
love your genderless body.

Barbie gets haughty, stands
at the urinal and won't sit
on the potty. Ken doll simps
for Israel & Saudi. This is *kung*

fu, not karate! Go down, Miss
Moses! Beam me up, Scotty!

36

When you wish upon a tsar,
wise men blunder from afar.
Holy fuck! Is that your truck?
Each tire is wider than the sky.

Watch it crush the electric car
flat as a flat earth pancake. Goodbye,
Columbus! Hello, Toledo!
I left my heart inside a tuxedo.

Est perdido, my libido.
Mark but this mosquito
on your cheek. I clap death
with one hand. Where I Aim

is where I Am, is my Apollo Credo.
Where I aim and don't give a damn.

I give you all of my selves,
forty million dead
red-blooded cells
ghost dancing on the head

of a sin to exterminate
the oppressor. And you
give me what? *POW!*
right in the kisser.

Eastertime, too.
You'd think by now
I wouldn't miss her.
But every day, I do.

Objects are more fractured than they appear.
Self-portrait in a Cracked Rearview Mirror

38

Endless summer
of our discontent.
Just follow where
the junky went.

Squad car stripped
on cinder blocks.
The bone trees drip
with melting cocks.

4/20—Never Forget!
hug 4 Life! Punk Snot Dead!
Be a Smart Bomb.
Use your warhead.

The only good Commie
is one that's read.

39

I'm pulling my fallen Father.
Pulling him up by the arm.
With both hands I'm pulling
a tough and stubborn weed

loose from hard earth, long
white roots ripping like stitches.
Well, I know what that means:
time to get a new Father.

Out here in the Far Field where
I let the unforgiven Papa waltz
round & round the same old faults.
Bullwhips crack the bitter air.

Trees bear strange fruit.
"Hands up!" Then shoot.

If you haven't failed yet,
it's because you're still trying.
"Hey, this bed is all wet!"
It's alright, ma, I'm only crying.

Death of fresh air sighing
all the way to the vault. Every school
a potential massacre. Every tribe a cult.
You! Yes, you! With the halo round

your bleating heart. It's all *your* fault!
Four roars and seven jeers ago. Now make
like a whip and smart. Turn a somersault
on the grassy knoll. The demolition is

under control. The sinking ship had no
captain. Its fleece was white as coal.

41

I pledge allegiance to the f ag.
I bark like a god in heat.
That funeral ghost was a southern flag.
Blather. Wince. Repeat.

I'm your best f iend. I put the need
in the needle. The up in smoke.
My braided bosom hides a roadside
bomb. My bombast is no joke.

I leave a body in stitches.
Or shred it to yellow ribbons
to tie around the old oak
tree. I'm violent but not evil. I open

the odor for you. Inside my revolver,
a lover. You know my aim is true.

42

Mind your *hoof!*
I think I'm coming
apart at the roof.
Is there a doctor

in my blouse?
Is there a carpenter
in the House
of the Holy

Moly Cannoli? Is *any*
body's Daddy home?!
Asses, asses, walls fall
down! I blame the many,

the proud. I think the Anthem
is too *goddamn* Loud!

43

The life of the mind is wasted on me.
I leave *Paradise Lost* in the parking lot.
Plan a zero-tolerance shopping spree.
Advance to NO! Get out of Hell free.

Pick a world, any maxed-out world.
In the Year of Our Lord & Taylor.
Who's afraid of Norman Mailer?
I AM the Jonestown Massacree!

I sing "Happy Birthday, Mr. President"
in the key of tease. Then spit one on the House
with extra sleaze. A finger lick of the Devil's
sympathy. Who owns Pennsylvania Avenue

IS Pennsylvania Avenue! Say "*Woo woo!*"
Now let's begin with "*Please.*"

44

"Violence begets violence!"
Christ *snaps!* me with a towel.
I respond with the sound of silence,
stitch of cross hairs on his brow.

How now scared cow? Heaven
is for tyrants! I hereby disavow
that celestial alliance. And crusade
instead for this Robo-Maid

as a miraculous appliance.
It sure as heck beats self-reliance.
You can tweak her tweeters
without defiance. Or if she hollers,

reroute her for compliance.
Easy as creation science!

45

Sitting here helping my fingernails grow.
Skating around my own mental rink.

"Hello" 's but a stone's throw
from the immanent brink.

The tape's running slow.
My lips aren't in sync.

All night I crow,
all day I blink.

Can't know!
Don't think!

Watch Aristotle
spin down the sink.

I pass Love the bottle.
And Love takes a drink.

46

He merely experimented, reality shot
amidst the jumble. Not scripted plots
of ABCs, guarantees, pretty please, wrapped
in a poetic skin disease. *It all Unknots*

in defiance of Death, summed up
the method obliquely. Creation tapped
fears, hall of cracked mirrors, until it broke
completely. Almost sweetly. Coffee cup

filled with tears. For years, a voice spoke
less and less concretely. In his diary
he wrote, three days before the end:
Neck-deep in the rival/viral hegemony. . .

It occurs to me I am the Enemy.
I am listening to myself again.

47

Cold rain. Coltrane.
Beating all my
coal trains
into words

that cut, slice, dice,
dismember
and decapitate. (*Great,*
but what about nice?

Remember?)
Nice is a gelded fate.
A gilded dream.
The gulled hem that

seams irreality to
a Love Supreme.

48

You may say I'm a screamer.
But I'm not the lonely one.
Simon Cowell says, "Act cute!"
I answer the teacher with a one

-arm salute. My skin suit
fits like a silicon glove. Been
driving around in pentagrams
since the Summer of Love.

I put the heart before the curse.
I open my purse inward to the Lord.
Nothing left to nurse. My other lemon
's a hearse. Quick to disperse.

But it only goes forward,
it's got no reverse.

49

"Sure as today hounds tomorrow,
free your mind
and an ass will follow.
Giddy-up!, Three of a Kind.

Let's duck this Sleepy Hollow.
Blinders leading the blind
feeding every bit they swallow."
"Whoa! Hold on there, big fella!

Or should I yell *'Stellaaah!'*?
Fact of the latter, it's your own
behind that's behind. Even a cappella
pays the piper. A loan is a loan

is a jawbone broken by a Whale.
Imagine it so proudly we fail."

50

It's in rain flames! Sorry
Sky. Starting motors,
I start to lie. I've lost my
mooring. One story

at a time. Such terrific
breakage. The meaning was
the wreckage. No one got
the message. No one even

tried. "Out of the way!"
they cried. "Worst thing
I've ever seen!" "No humanity."
One lady screamed,

"I can't even talk! In fact,
I can hardly breathe."

51

Above all, know what I mean,
not what I say. Remember the milk
of human kindness wasn't spilt
in a day. Lather ye soapsuds

while ye may. Keep a clean rose.
Don't let the Instagram go up the nose.
Don't let your Wiki leak. Before every
school shooting, remember to prey.

Remember the Alamo! Remember
the Maine! Remember the words
of the old Negro spiritual: "No pain,
no gain." The Lord is your shepherd.

Now be a good sheep. *WAKE UP!*
And let me sleep.

$$ Poet Is Punk & Poetry Is Play $$

The arrangement is versatile, but cannot be truncated. Remove one line, one phrase, and you've pulled the pin- from the eapple. *Snapple!* Now what the fuck are you going to do? Watch it topple like *Jenga!*, I guess. And when it does you remove another sock, slingshot it across the room, spin the revolver, and go again. I'm out back, under a gibbous moon, howling "*Wolf!*" in a crowded fire. Scared sacred. Still learning how to be abstract, yet still intact. Digging with a shovel, not a pen. I stomp on the back of the rusty blade, slice into cold, hard Fact. Slick incisive sound, almost wet, with a faint scrape of metal. Down through guts and gravel. Igneous and malachite taken for granite. Remnants of Pop Top and Pull Tab *(What in Dog's name were you thinking?!)* Substrata of progress and sin. The aim of the game is to find out how to begin. The ending's all the same to me. I go to sleep eventually, too, you know. Make some Zzzzs. On beyond zebra. Leave residue of ash. Footprint of Cash. Whirlpool of words spinning down the brain. Land at

Plymouth Rock and spray my name. Wage a trillion dollar bash! Hulk *SMASH!* Kick some sage and burn their ass. For some California grass. Somewhere wages and wages hence, I shall be selling this with a tie: *"Robert Hass* gave me *Sorbet Rash!"* Right on my Buster Keaton. It only hurts when I'm eatin', and I'm eatin' all the time. Constantly chewing. Mostly mooing and booing all the mewing and ewing, too much straight cueing, spewing from your one-track line. What a drag it is getting told the same thing thrice! Why, that's colder than ICE! Like shoot first, then say *Freeze!* Talk about a snow job in Hell. What am I? The fuckin' drive-thru intercom at Mickey D's? Huh? Your mother's ear? Huh? Tough guy? No wonder Rover took over and gave a bone of his own. Is that a smart phone vibrating in your pocket? Or are you just glad to read me? High sign of Democracy! RIPs an after-blast of Hypocrisy. Jesus Chrysler, big as a Whale! American flag Made in China, girl! Into the cardiac night! Take two lefts and make a right! "Stop texting and *Drive!*" he sd. *"LOOK OUT! for that blasted nymph of regret!"*. . . Annnd *Cut!/*

These Sonnets like soldiers come pre-assembled.
Made to serve. Ready to order. At least three
sides to every border. Just follow the bouncing
Skull. Sing along for the tribe. The more looney
the tuney the merrier! Be not the bridge but the
Great Divide. Let Distraction be your guide.
Spectacle is Sheen and demands to be seen.
"Attention, shoppers, is required!" Meaning takes
a back seat and steams. "Can't see the clitoris for
the sleaze!" This is the image I get while
masticating at the screen. Coming clean. Every
last nerve, down to the live wire. And won't settle
for some now-you-see-it-now-you-don't Side-
show of the Free. No way, José. We're all out of
Please. I'm a frayed knot, Madam. Odor of bare
necessities. It's do or die or did I sneeze? If X were
Y, what a breeze. Get a grip! Now *squeeeze.*
Smoke skin coils in the trees. Adam had'em:
Enemies.

Acknowledgements

Grateful acknowledgement is made to the editors of the following publications where some of these poems, sometimes in a slightly different form, first found a home:

Eunoia Review: American Sonnet "12" and "34"

frak\ture: American Sonnet "39"

Home Planet News: American Sonnet "5"; "36"; and "50"

Packingtown Review: American Sonnet "8" (published as "A Little Push")

Synchronized Chaos: American Sonnet "45" (published as "American Sonnet")

What Rough Beast: American Sonnet "9" (published as "My Latest Flame")

Cover art by Xihan Li

Special thanks to Don Bertschman and Shelley Xiuli Tong, each of whom believed in, encouraged, read through, edited, and helped shape this manuscript at critical stages in its evolution. Safe to say, this collection would not exist without them.

And to Matt Morris, for bringing it all to light.

John Martino is a poet, photographer, and educator originally from Glassport, Pennsylvania. After earning a PhD in English Literature at West Virginia University, he relocated to Boston, working as an Associate Professor at Fisher College and creatively pursuing film-based black & white street photography. Since June 2016, he has lived primarily in Hong Kong with his partner, Xiuli. An appreciation for some of what was happening in American poetry between 2005 and 2015 reignited his interest in the medium. Martino traces his poetic roots to the lyrical wordsmiths he obsessed over as a youth: "Around the age of 10, I became aware that language could be deployed creatively, poetically, elliptically via the pop and rock songs I was listening to, first on the radio, then on the many recordings I began to collect. I didn't explore poetry-poetry, Wordsworth et al., until I was a university undergrad." Since 2019, Martino's poems have appeared in more than 25 publications. *American Sonnet* (Half Inch Press) is his debut poetry collection. Its first complete incarnation as 51 "little songs" was drafted during a 10-month stay in San Francisco. Six years later, in Marseille, France, the manuscript was edited and remixed to its current playlist.

www.ingramcontent.com/pod-product-compliance
Lightning Source LLC
Chambersburg PA
CBHW071949100426
42736CB00042B/2601